This Book Belongs a:

_____

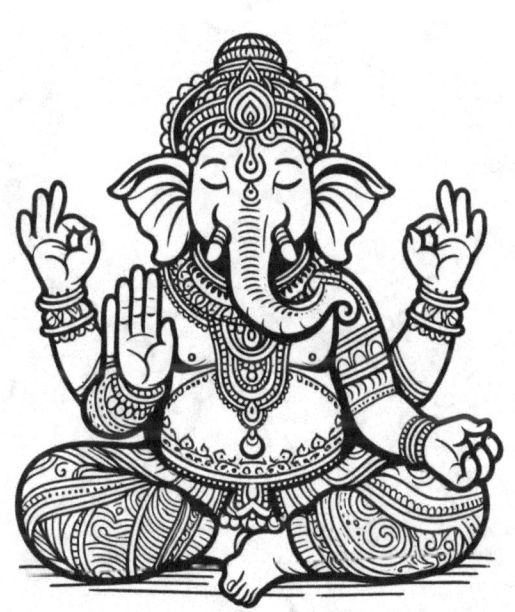

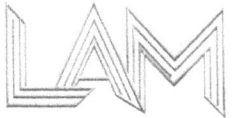

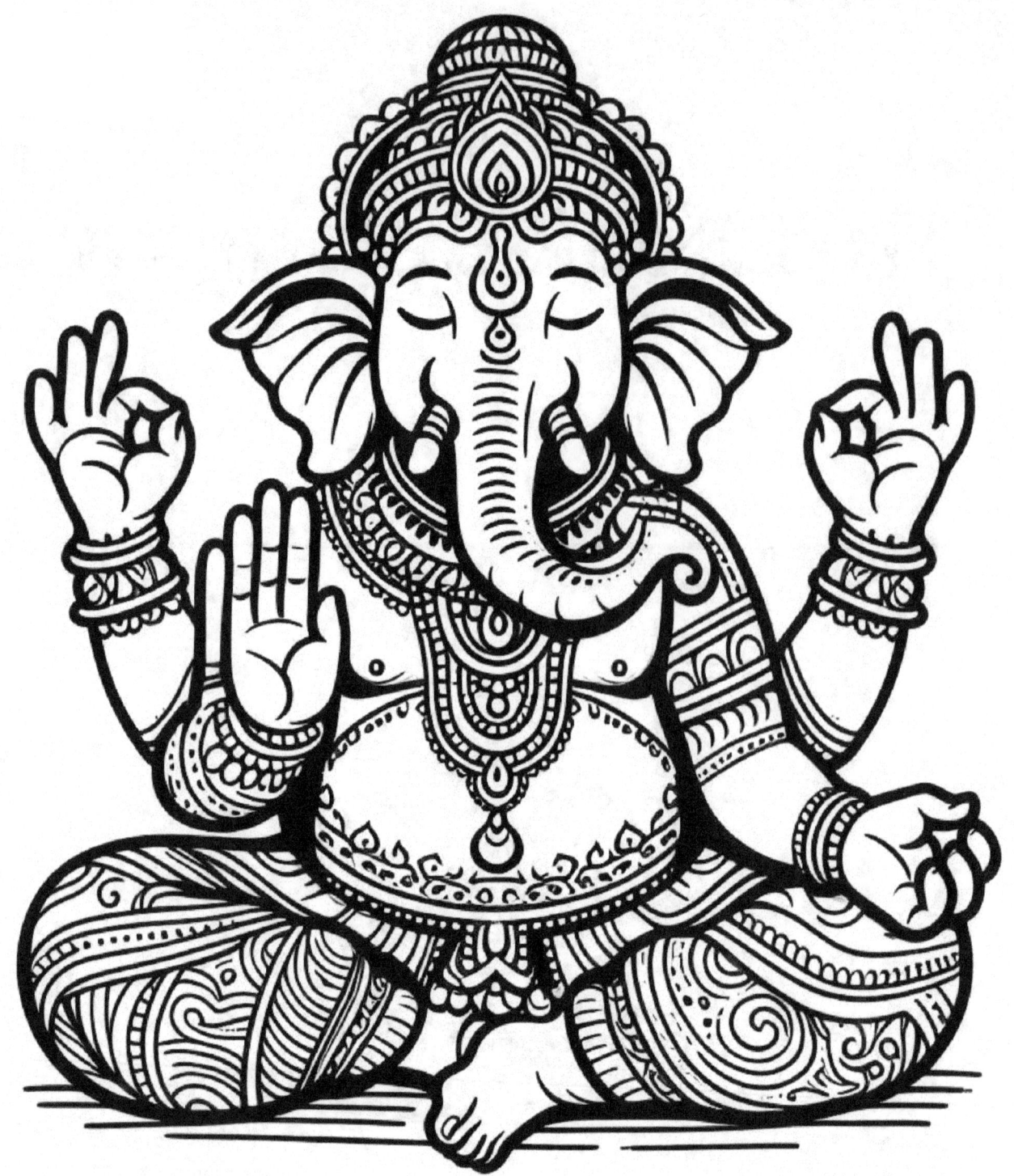

Ganesha – Lord of obstacles

Ganesha is the lord of obstacles. Due to her youthful and protective characteristic, she is present in the daily lives of a large part of the Hindu population and is one of the most popular Indian gods in the world. The elephant head is his trademark. At the same time, he bestows wisdom and luck to remove obstacles from life, whether in a marriage or a business venture. However, it can also put up obstacles in order to prevent someone from going down the wrong path.

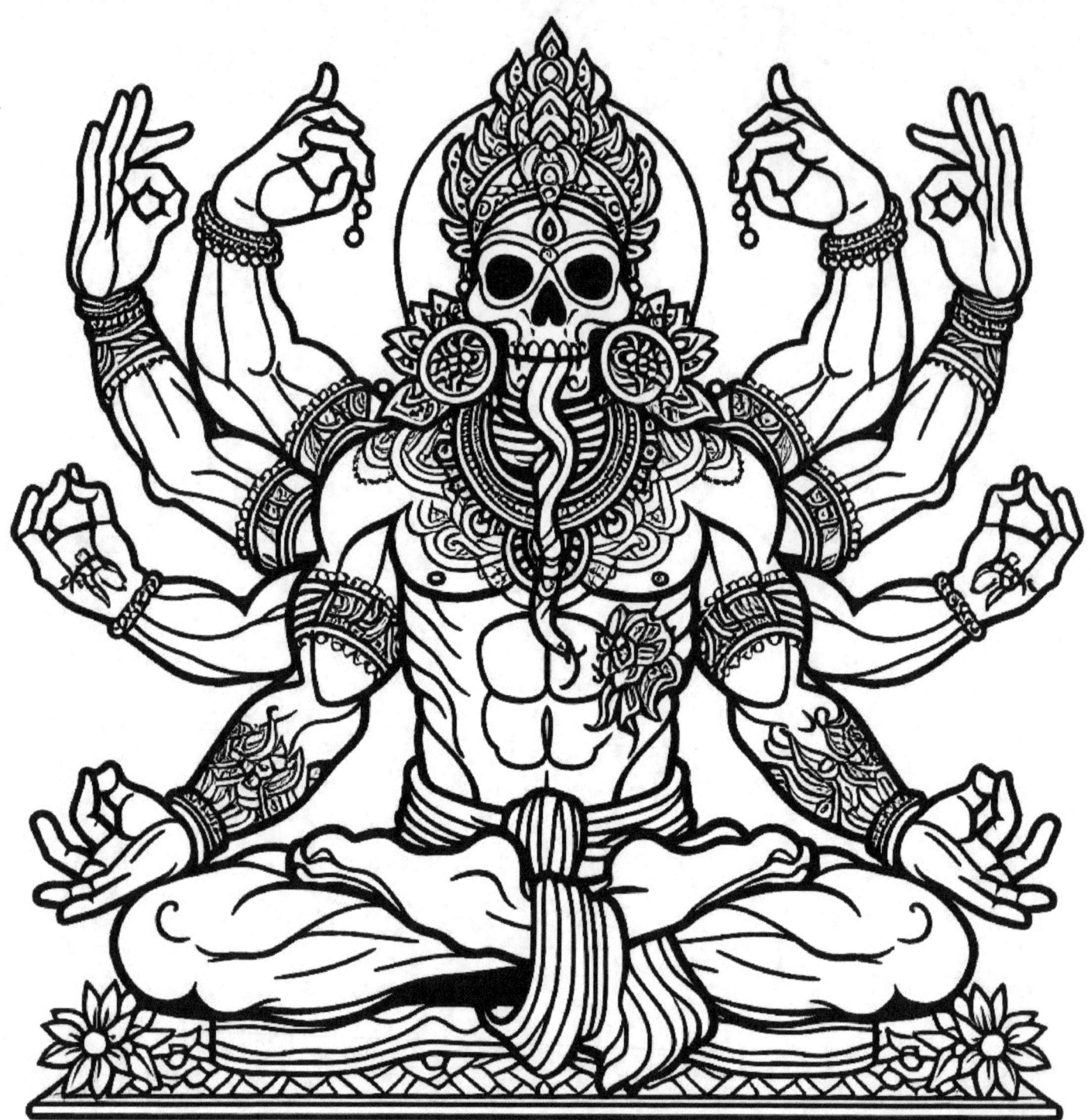

Yama – god of death

Yama, described in the first inscription of the Vedas, the Samsara, is the god of death. Therefore, he is the ruler of the Hindu underworld and thus meting out punishments to the dead according to their sins in their carnal lives. However, even though he is the controller of the underworld, he is still at the mercy of Shiva and Vashnu, the greatest controllers of the Hindu universe. In conclusion, Yama is often depicted as a blue man, who holds an apple and a noose and rides a buffalo.

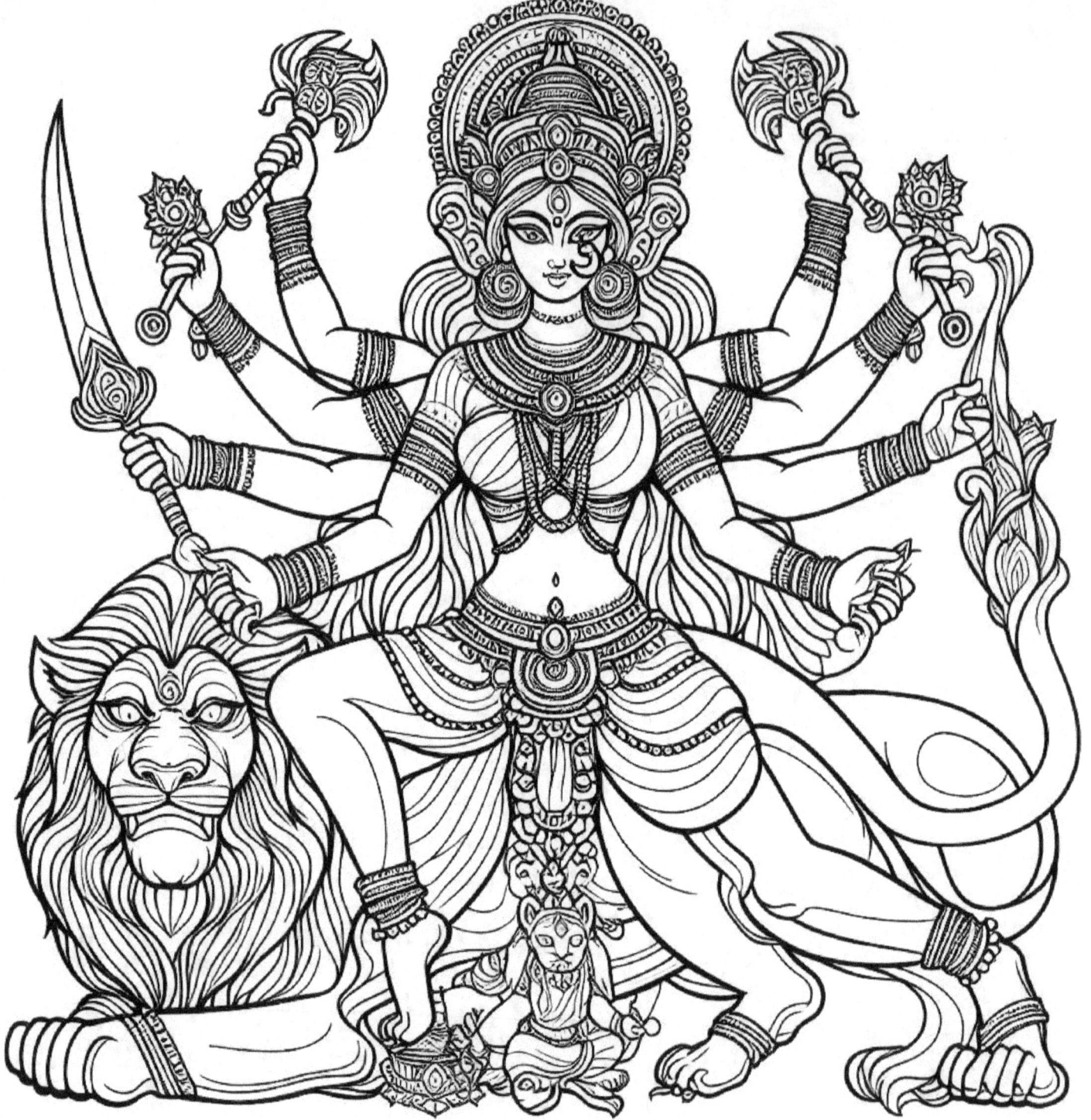

Durga – protective goddess

Durga, or also known as Amba and Bravani, is the divine mother among the Indian gods, she protects all the righteous who have bravery in their hearts. Not only is she the primordial feminine principle, but she is also the mother progenitor of the entire universe. She is invincible and always fights against evil. Their mission is always to overcome evil in order to achieve good and prosperity. In this way, she is depicted with eight arms carrying weapons to confront evil in all corners of the world.

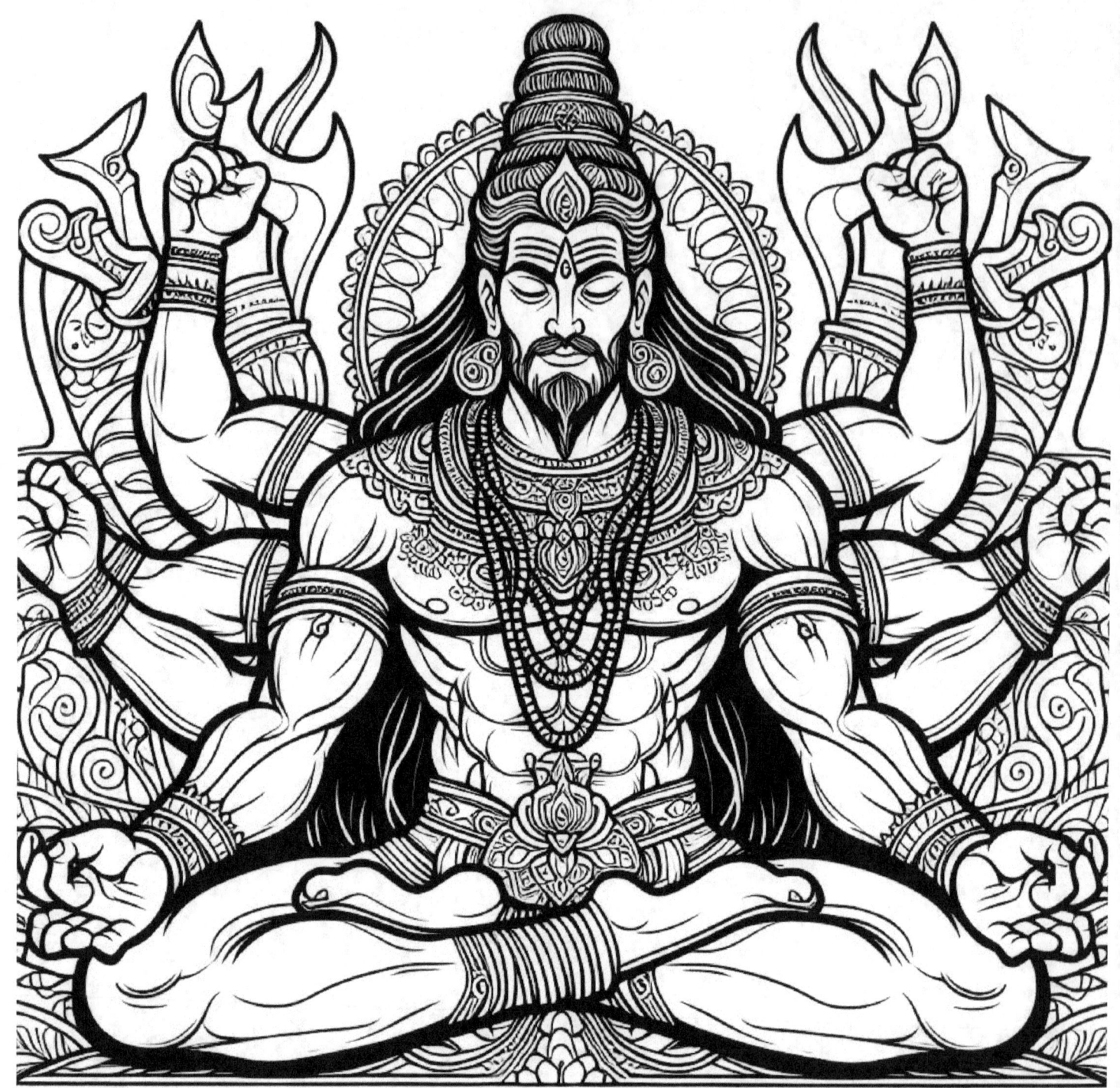

Kartikeya – god of war

Kartikeya is the god of war and the brother of Ganesha and the son of Shiva and Parvati. Tarak is a demon who could only be defeated by a son of Shiva. And that was the mission of Kartikeya, who was born with this goal. Therefore, he was the commander of the divine forces in the battle against evil. Lastly, he is usually depicted as a handsome man, carrying weapons and riding a peacock. But in some versions it has six heads and twelve arms.

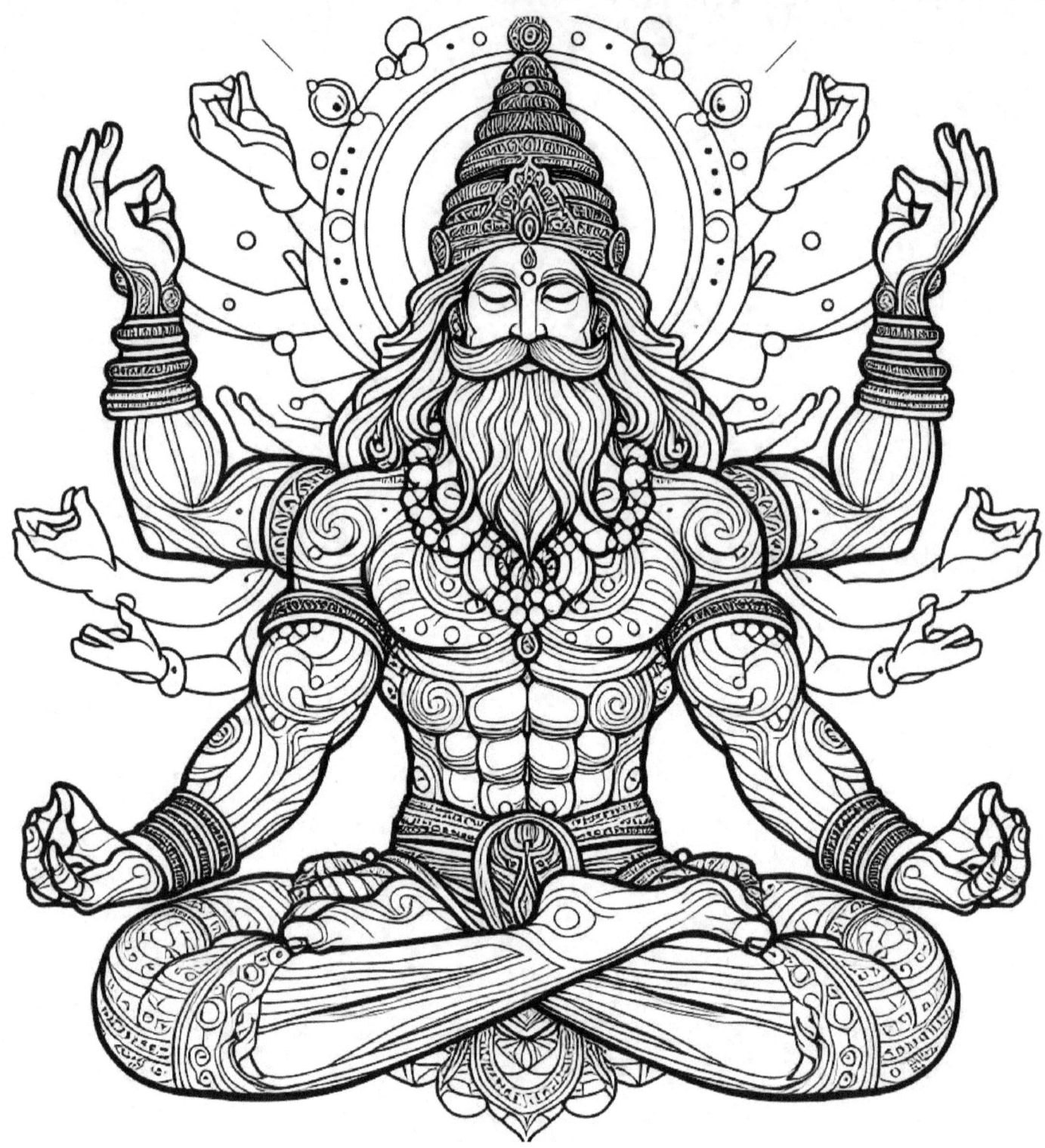

Varuna – god of immortality

Varuna, the guardian of immortality, was once a deity similar to Vishnu. However, with the changes in the Hindu religion, he became a sea deity. In addition, it is depicted as a yellow-skinned man who wears golden armor and has four arms, usually mounted on an animal with land and sea features.

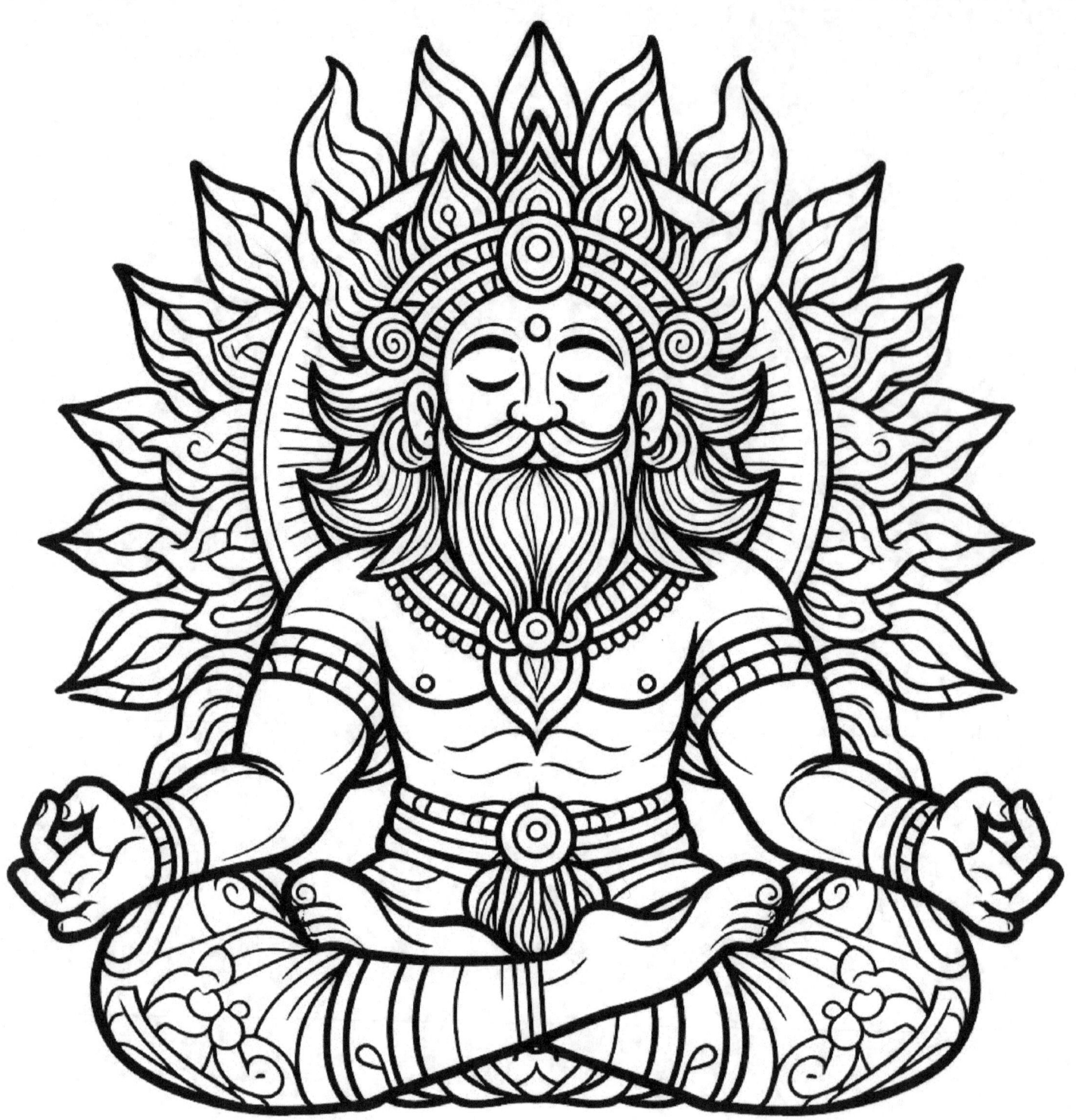

Surya – sun god

Surya is the god of the sun, so he dwelt in the solar sphere and his realm extended as far as the sun's rays touched. Also, Sunday, the solar day, is the day dedicated to Surya in which devotees eat only one meal. It is at this time that they make pleas for health and protection from nightmares.

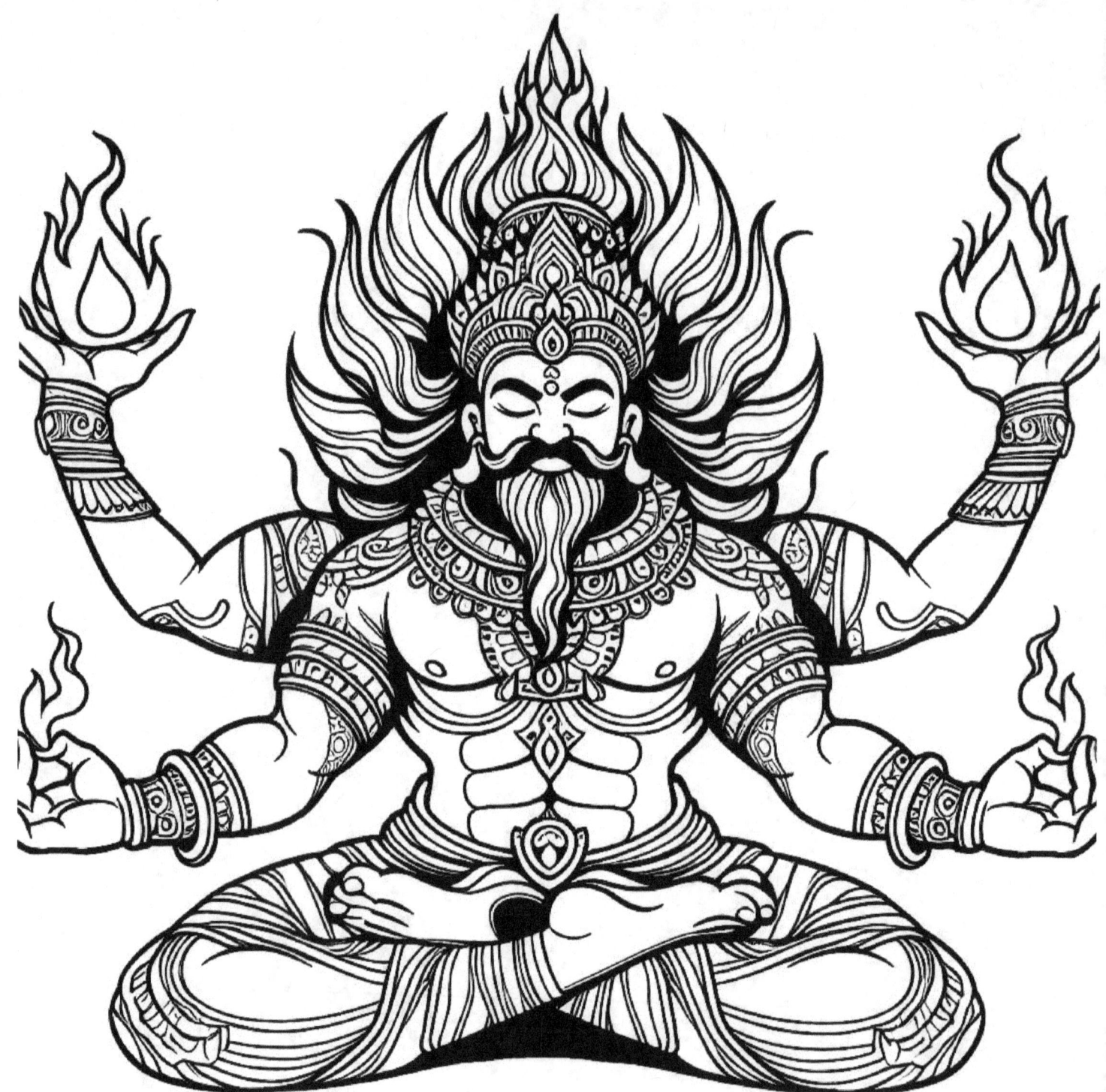

Agni – god of fire

According to Vedic mythology, Agni is second in power behind Indra, his twin brother. He is in everyone's heart and is the spark of life. As well as the messenger of the gods and acceptor of sacrifices. It is the representation of fire. In this way, it has ten mothers and two fathers who represent the ten fingers of the man and the two sticks that rub together to make the fire.

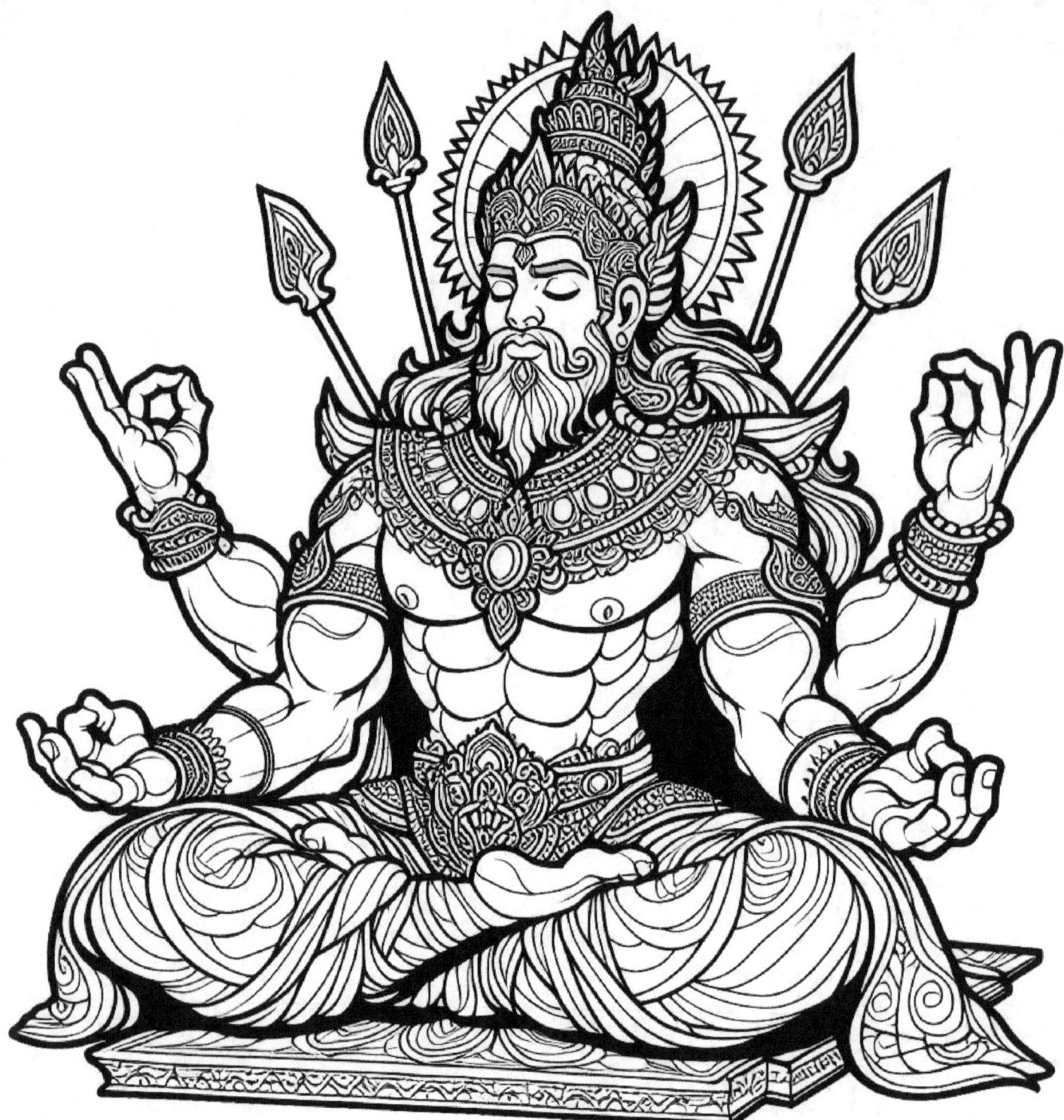

Indra – god of war

Indra is one of the first Indian gods of the Vedic age, by the way the most important of all. In addition, his depiction is compared to that of other European mythologies such as Zeus or Odin, as he possesses lightning as one of his weapons. It usually appears mounted on a white elephant and has four arms. It is the god responsible for the defeat of the supreme evil Vritra, who is responsible for the droughts. On the other hand, Indra is responsible for rivers and rainfall.

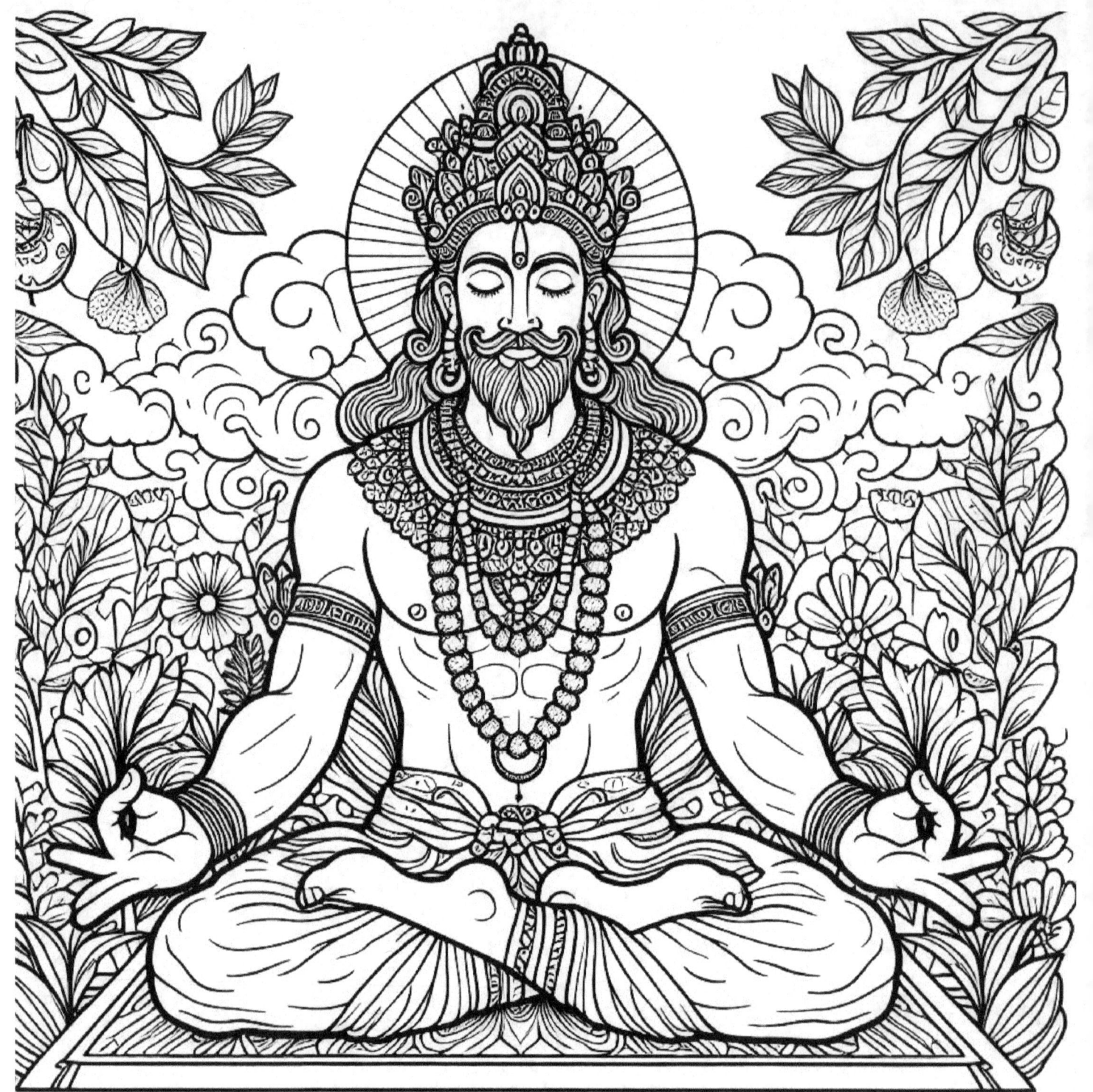

Brahma – god of creation

Brahma is the first god of the Hindu male Trinity, also called the Trideva. He is the god of creation and is considered one of the major Indian gods. Above all, he is responsible for the creation of the universe, especially when it is destroyed by Shiva. Despite this, its function goes much further, as Brahma is also considered the god of music. Regarding his physical representation, he is usually seen with four arms and four heads.

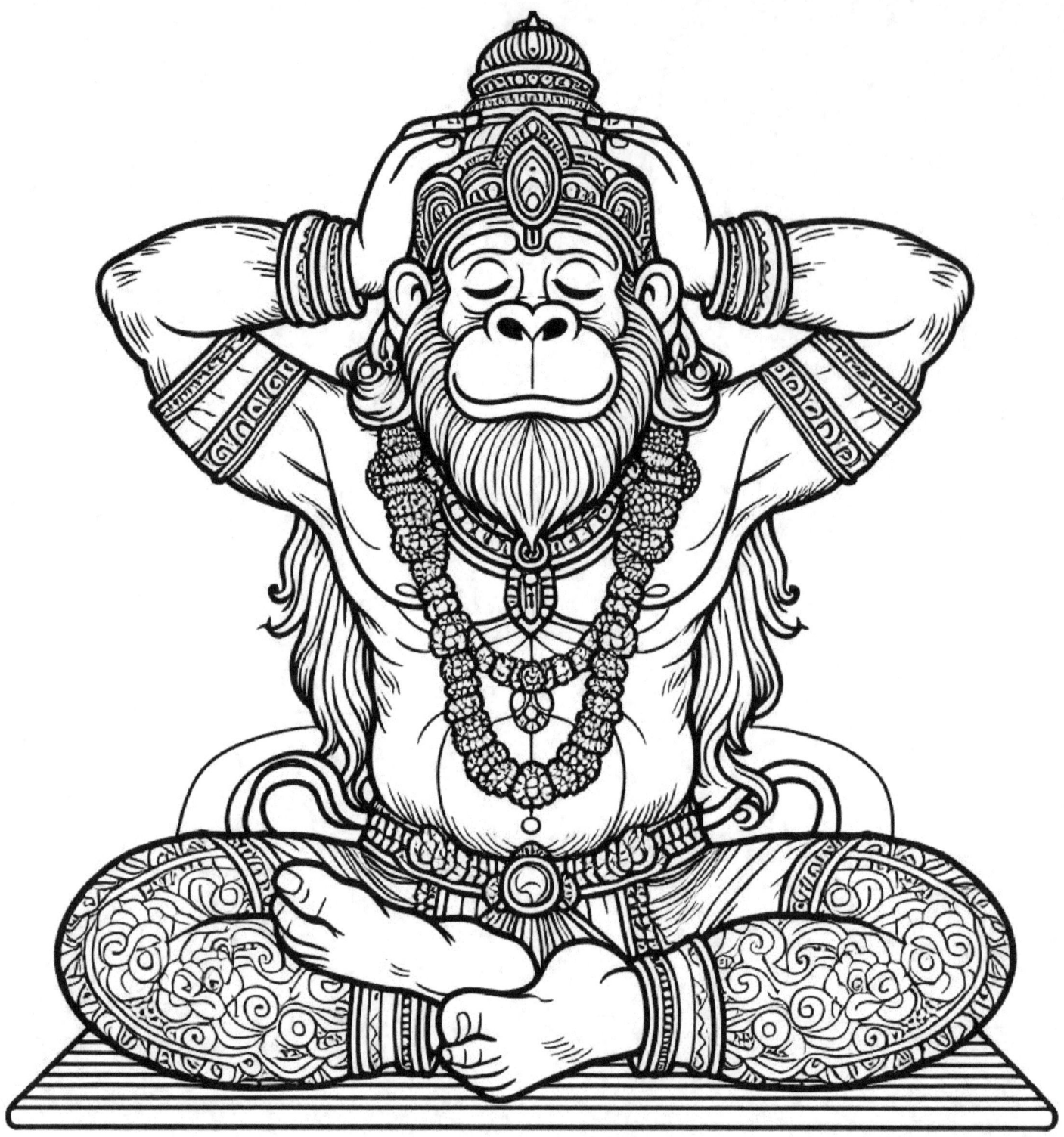

Hanuman – Symbol of strength and devotion

Have you ever heard of the god of impossible causes? Among the Indian gods, this is Hanuman, the one who reminds us that in everyone there is unlimited power and that they are capable of confronting it. But when is he remembered? Certainly when you're in tough times. The god, symbol of strength and devotion, is also found in the classic epic poem "Ramayana". Together with Rama he fights against evil. The monkey god, as he is also known, has several shrines in his honor in India.

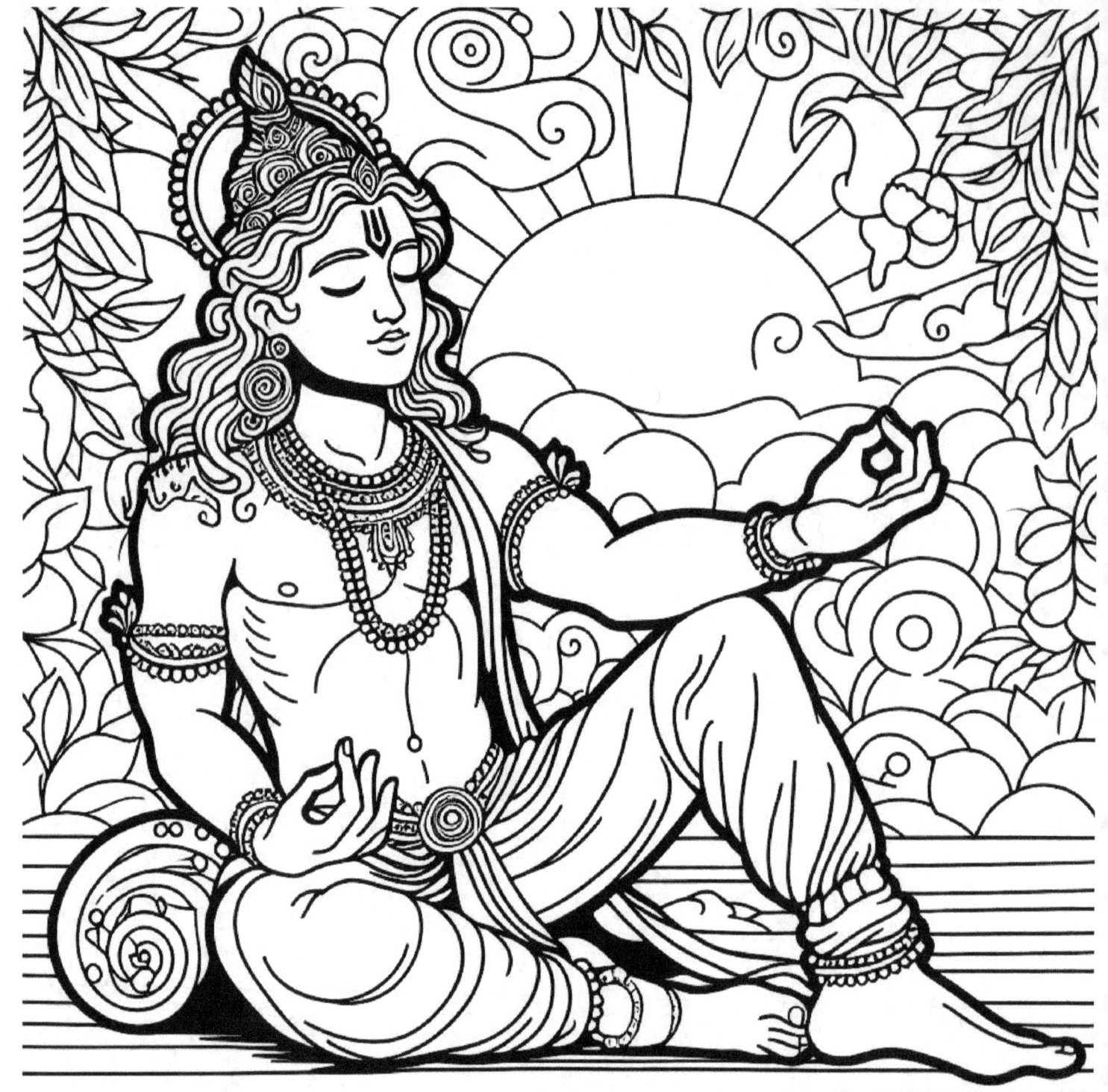

Kṛṣṇa – god of devotion

Kṛṣṇa, the god of devotion, is one of the forms that Vishnu takes. There are those who dare to say that certainly, this form is one of the most powerful incarnations of Hindu mythology. Anyone who practices yoga and meditation has heard a lot about this god of devotion. He is the one who brings balance, divine joy, and love. Their main instrument of seduction is the flute. This mark is registered in its personification.

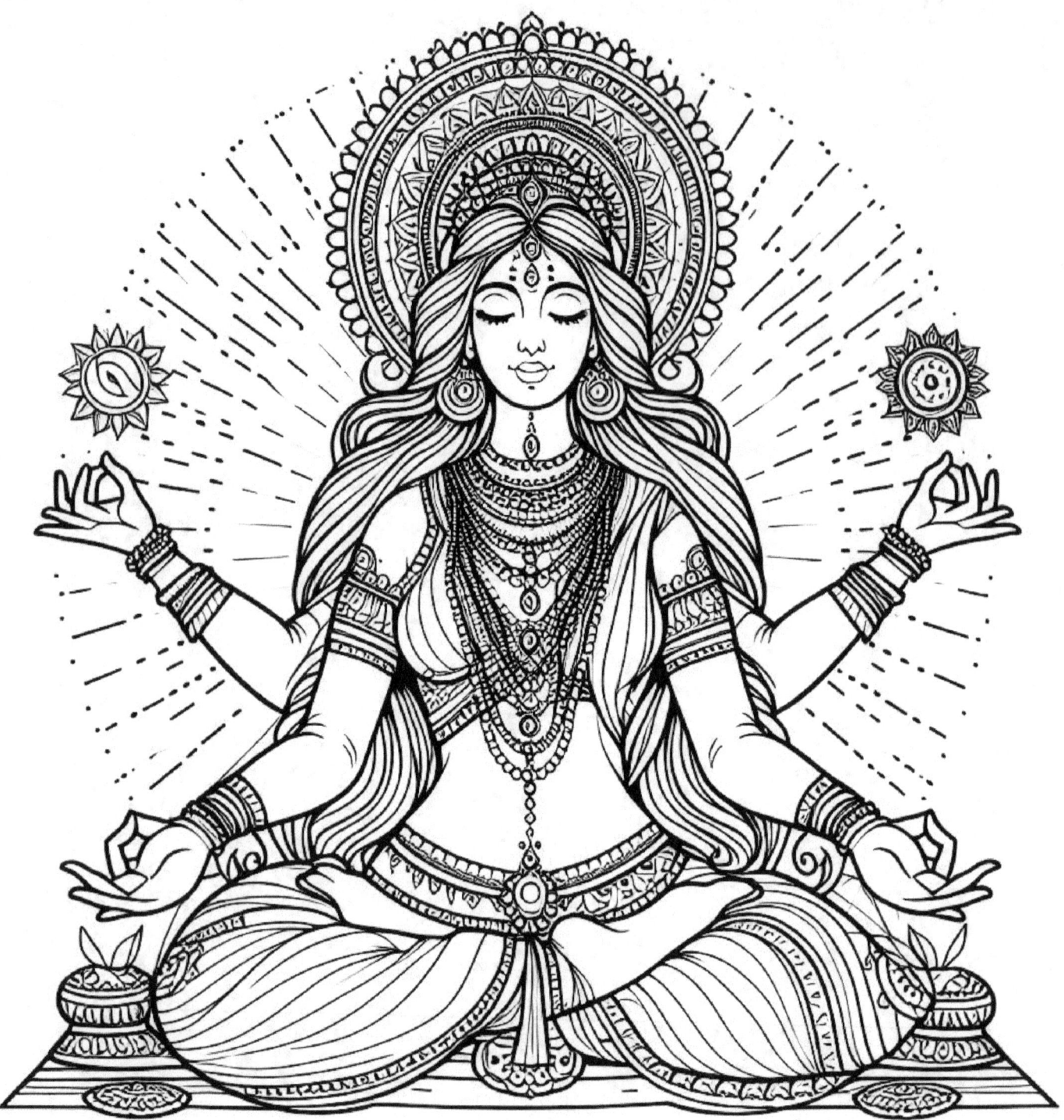

Shákti – The Great Mother

Shakti is the supreme mother, the great divine mother. Its psycho-spiritual force is popularly represented by Kundalini Shakti. It manifests on earth in the form of the goddesses Saraswati, Parvati, and Lakshmi, wives of Brahma, Shiva, and Lakshmi, respectively, who form the female Trinity of Hinduism, also called Tridevi.

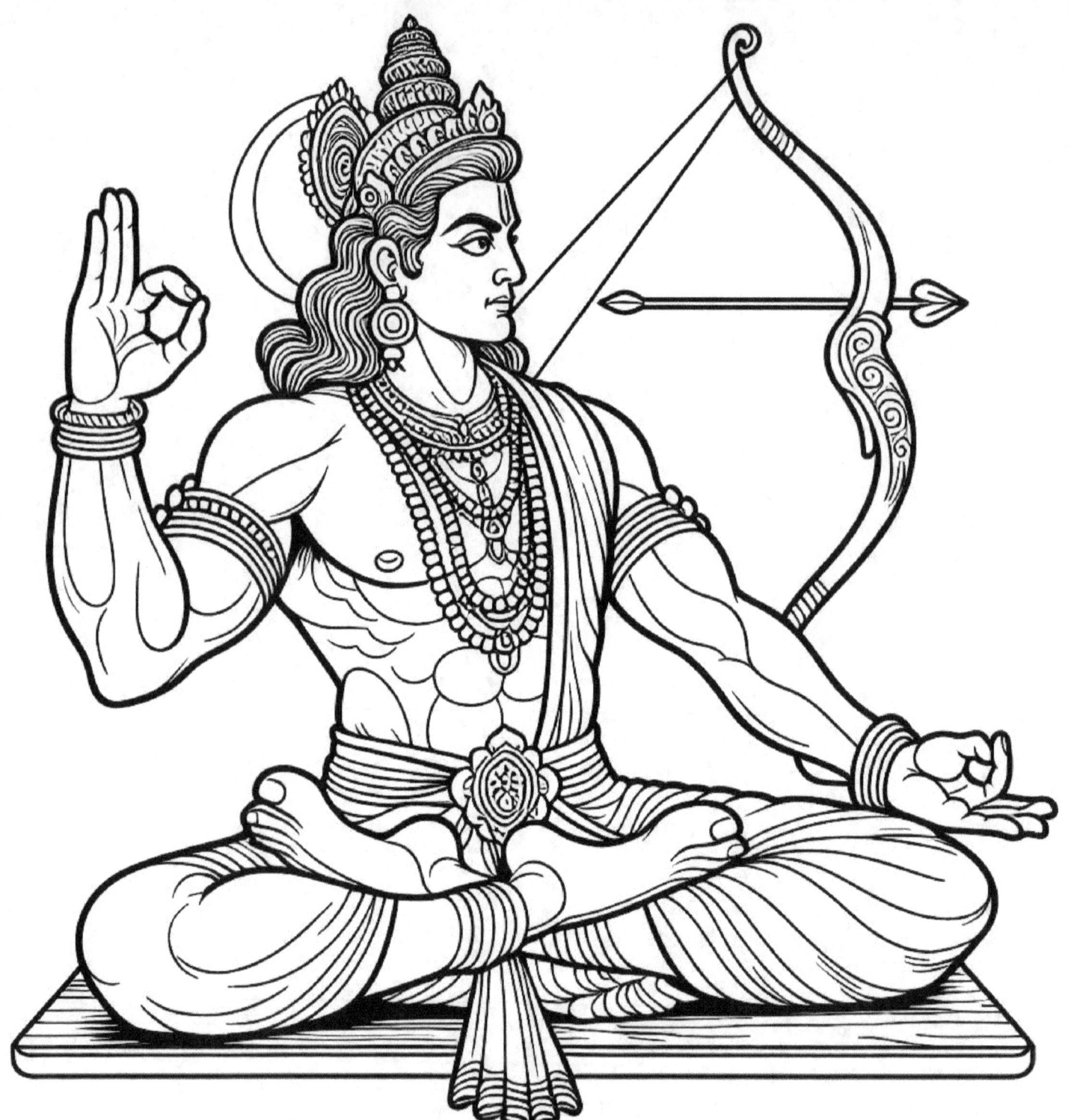

Rama – Model of Action and Virtue

Rama is also one of the forms that Vishnu takes and this avatar becomes the perfect embodiment of humanity. Therefore, he is the god of action and virtue whose story is described in the epic tale Ramayana. Like other Indian gods, he has several devotees. Let's say that his main reference is the Indian festival of lights held in his devotion.

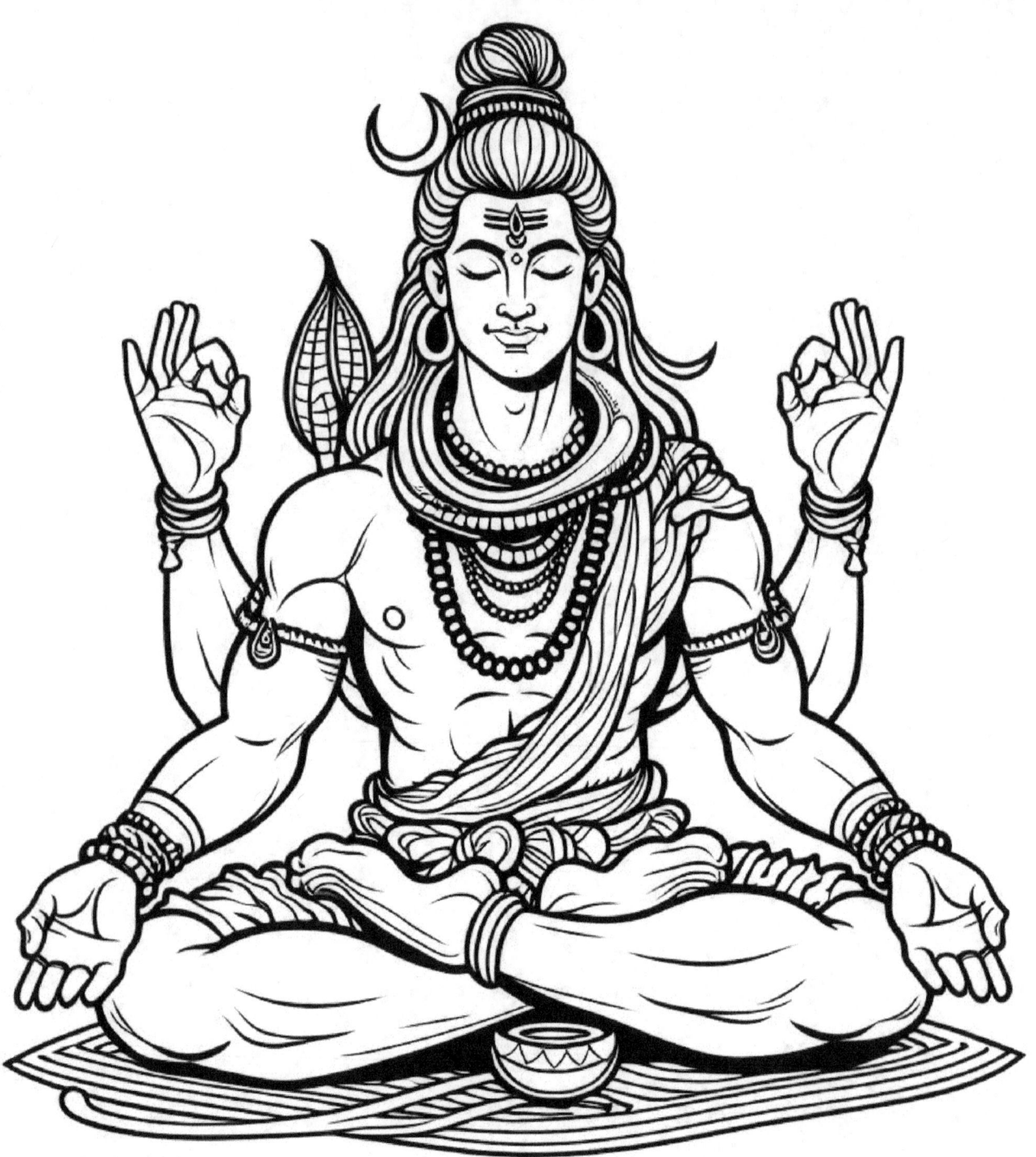

Shiva – god of destruction

You have already seen that Brahma is the creation of life and Vishnu is the preservation of life. Then Shiva came to be the destruction of life and complete the Hindu Trinity. Despite his features, Shiva is considered to be very quiet and few harbor anger against him. After all, it also protects from evil. Thus he can bring not only chaos, but also order. One of its main characteristics is, in each cycle, to destroy the universe.

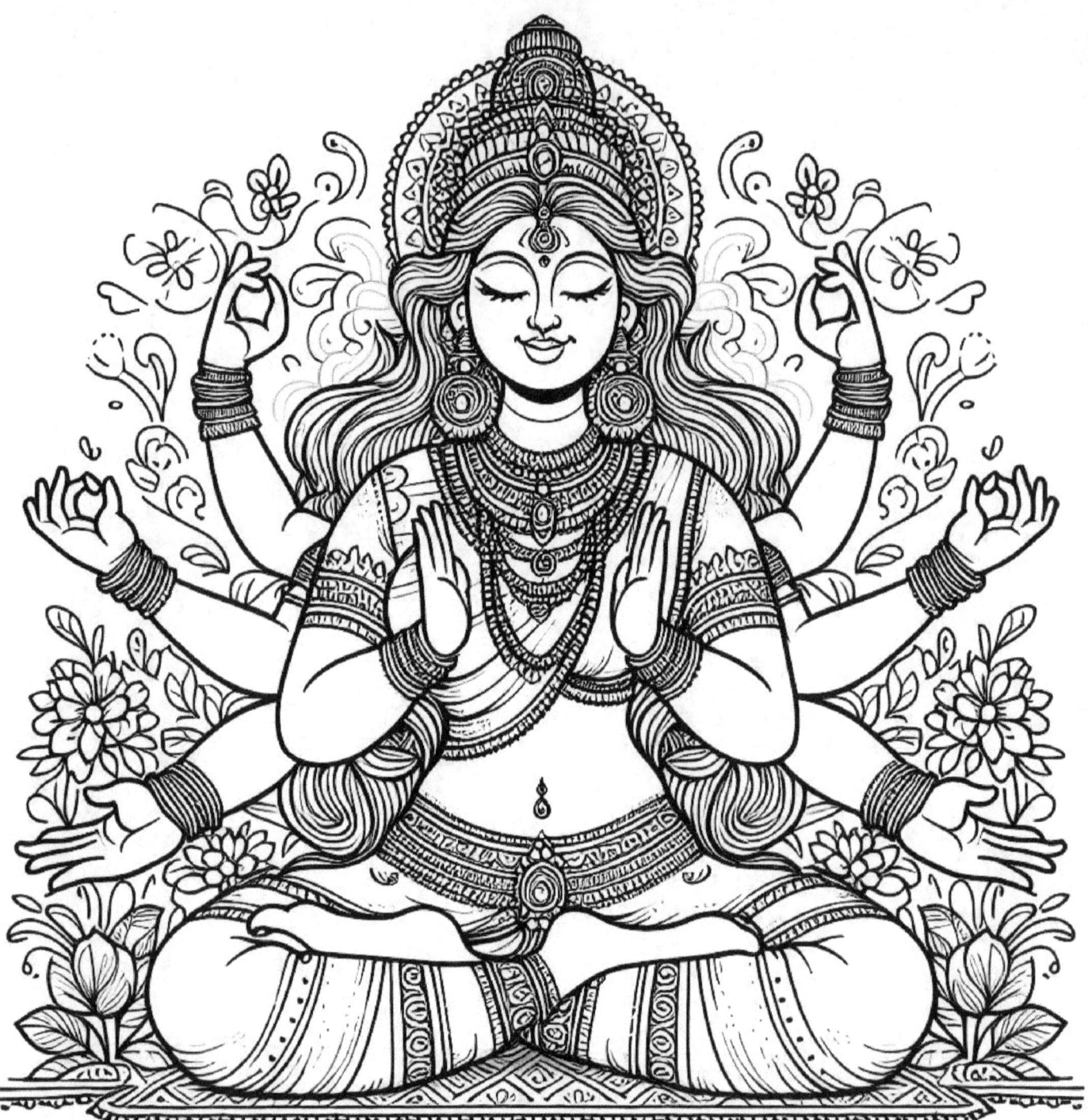

Lakshmi – goddess of money and wealth

Goddess of wealth, prosperity, and fortune. In some situations she is also the goddess of beauty and purity. This is Lakshmi, a goddess always sought after by those who are struggling financially and need a relief. It is not for nothing that she is one of the most popular among the Indian gods in India. A beautiful and graceful woman with four golden arms (representing wealth) and who distributes coins.

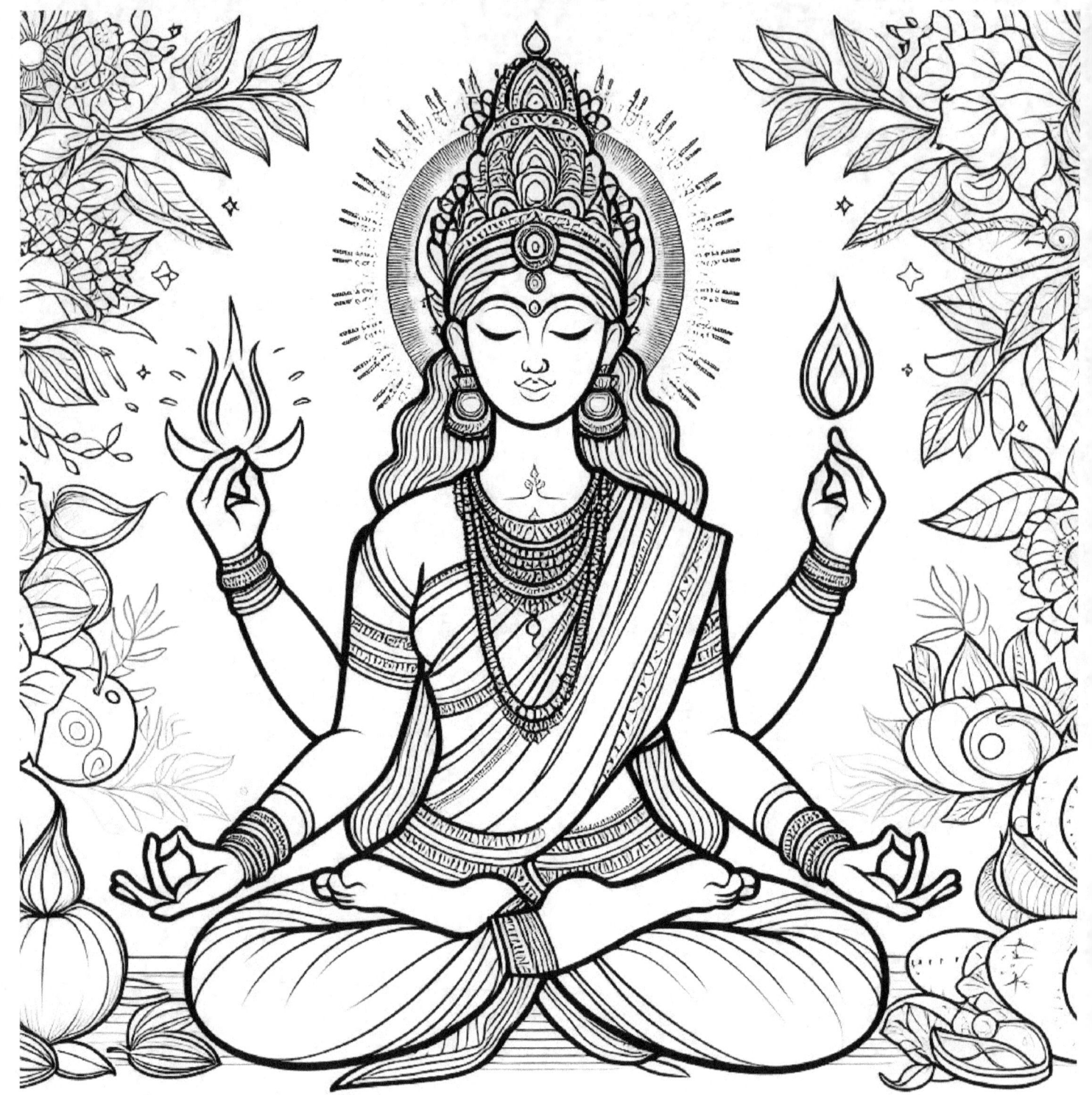

Saraswati – goddess of wisdom

Saraswati is one of the three great Hindu goddesses, that is, she is in the Trivedi. She is recognized as the goddess of wisdom, but carries other attributes as the goddess of writing, art, music, and knowledge. Therefore, she is much adored by her followers when they seek in their lives a lot of understanding and knowledge. In worship there is always talk of wisdom. Wife of Brahma and mother of Vedas. Thus, she is always represented as a beautiful woman with four arms and many jewels.

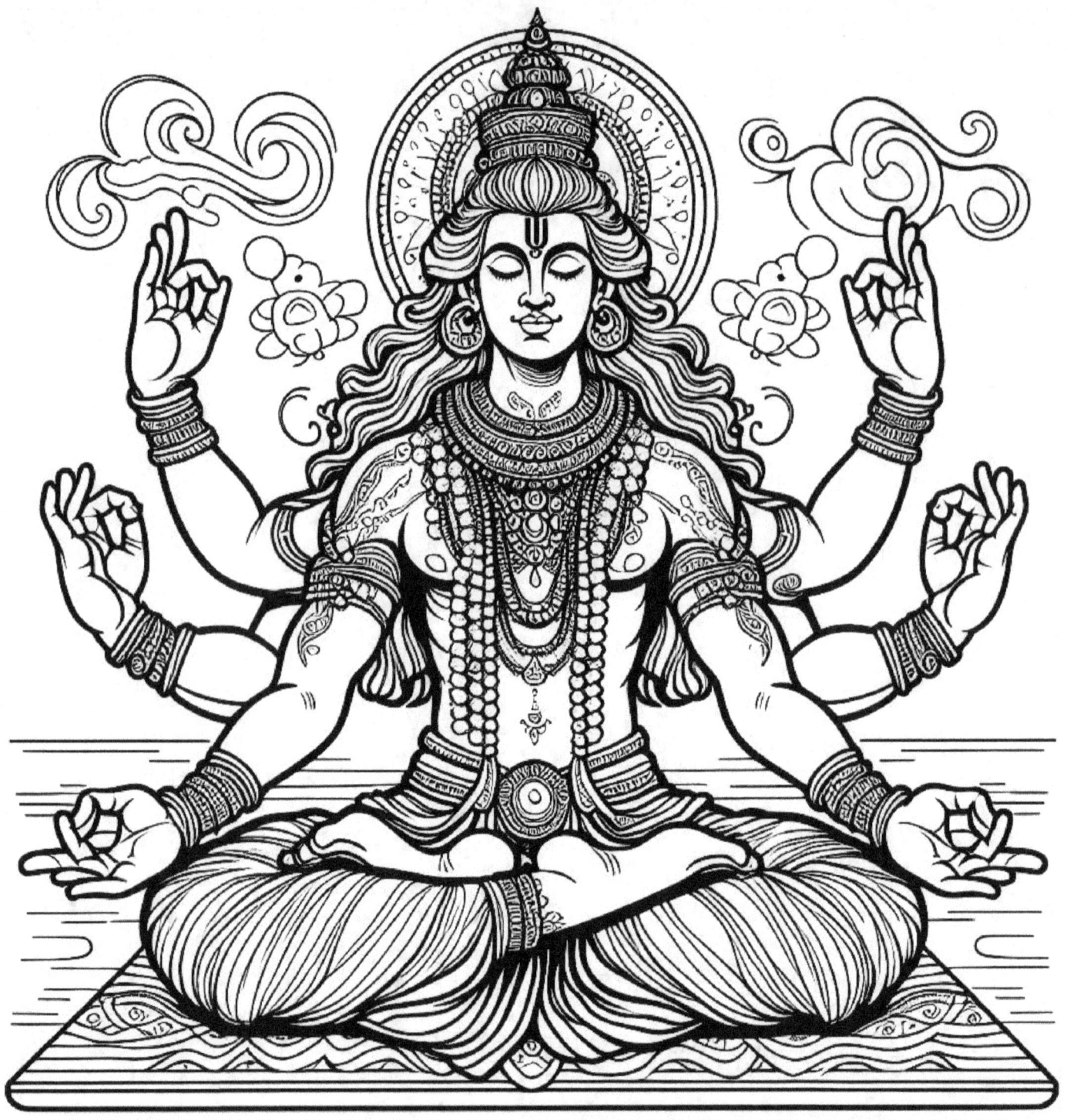

Vishnu – god of preservation

Together with Brahma and Shiva, Vishnu completes the Hindu Trinity. He is responsible for keeping the universe and Dharma (dignified and righteous behavior) in balance. With the principles of truth, righteousness, and order he preserves the natural world. Physically, he presents himself with a light blue skin, also with four arms and floating on a serpent of a thousand heads.

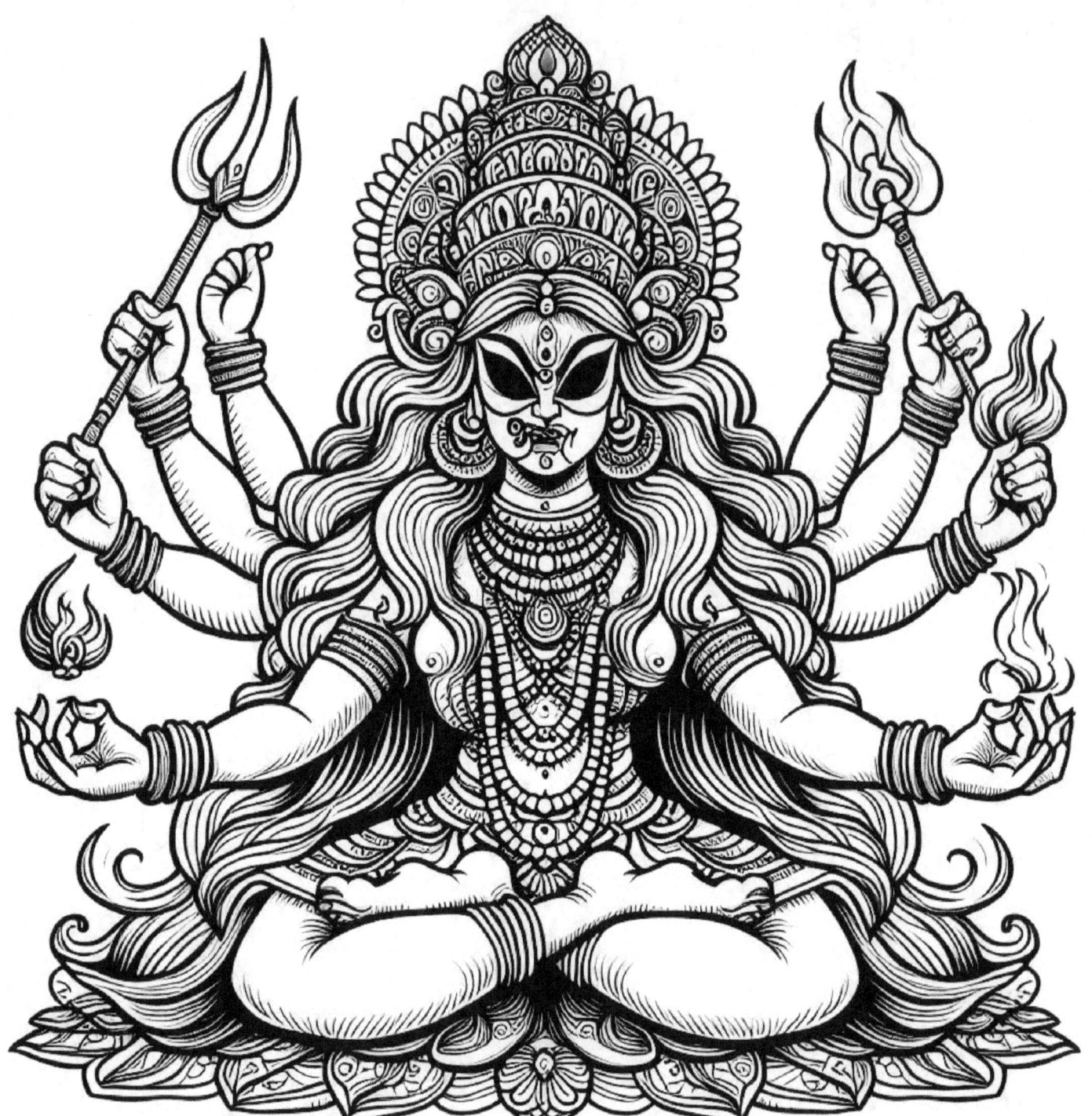

Kali – The Furious Mother of Time

Kali is one of the forms of Shakti (power), just like Tridevi. However, this form is fierce and violent and is depicted with a necklace of heads, eight arms, eight legs, and the head of Shiva. Do you know what is the greatest enemy of all humans and that destroys many lives? It's the ego. So he is the combat mission of Kali, the furious mother of time of the Indian gods and who has a natural strength to destroy everything.

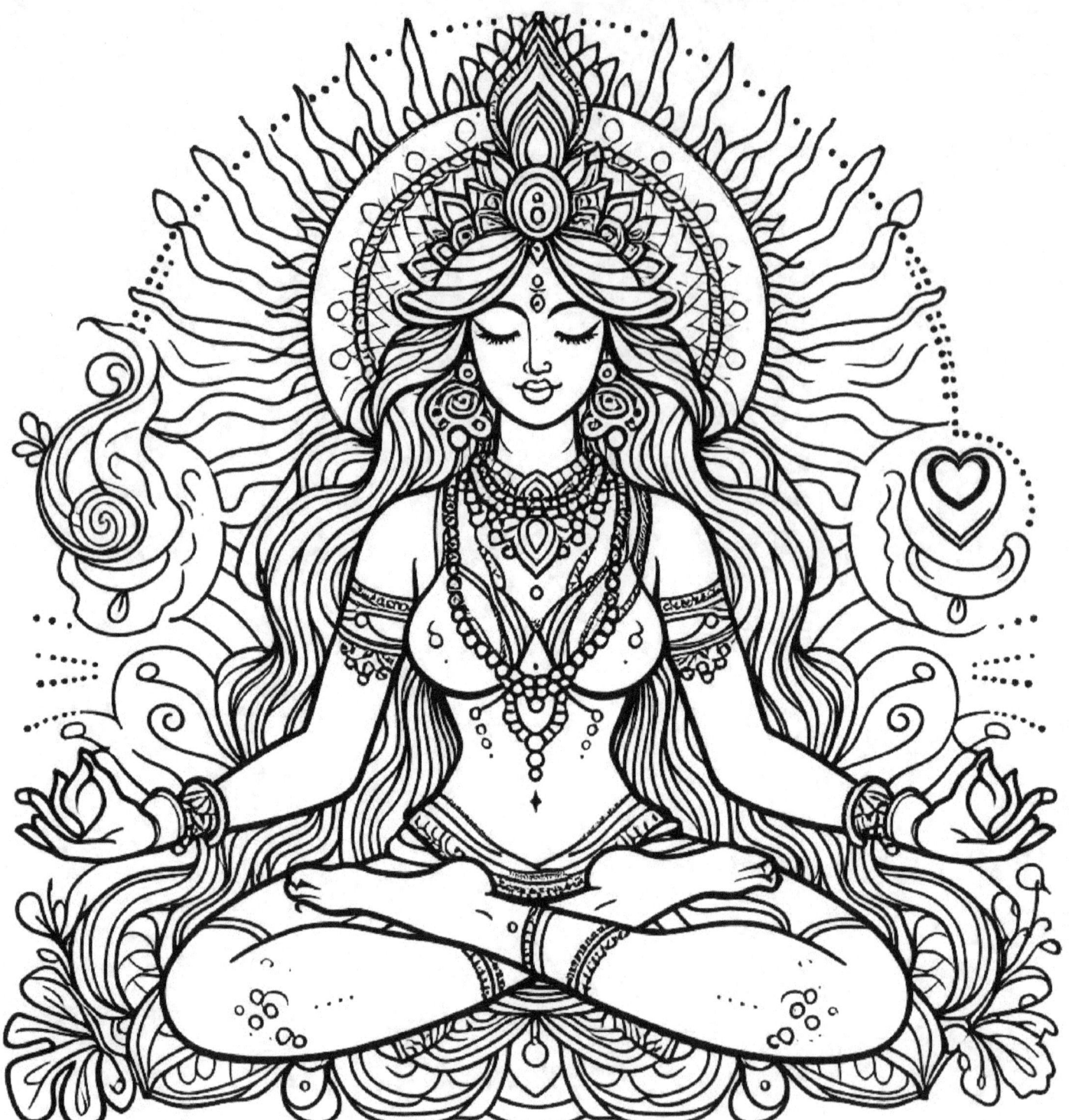

Parvati – goddess of love and fertility

Parvati is another of the goddesses of Tridevi, that is, one of the three great Hindu goddesses. She is the wife of Shiva and the mother of Ganesha and Kartikeya. Known as the goddess of love and fertility, she brings beauty and sustenance to marriage. At the same time, he fights to fight the demons. Parvati is, according to Shaktism, the source of Shiva's power. Physically there are two representations: with her husband she has two arms; But without it, she has four or even eight arms.